VOLUME 16

SING WITH THE CHOIR

AUDIO INCLUDED

THE GREATEST SHOWMAN

PLAYBACK+
Speed • Pitch • Balance • Loop

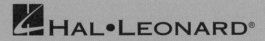

To access audio visit:
www.halleonard.com/mylibrary

Enter Code
2925-2458-3652-2053

ISBN 978-1-5400-5969-7

HAL•LEONARD®

Visit Hal Leonard Online at
www.halleonard.com

Contact us:
Hal Leonard
7777 West Bluemound Road
Milwaukee, WI 53213
Email: info@halleonard.com

In Europe, contact:
Hal Leonard Europe Limited
42 Wigmore Street
Marylebone, London, W1U 2RN
Email: info@halleonardeurope.com

In Australia, contact:
Hal Leonard Australia Pty. Ltd.
4 Lentara Court
Cheltenham, Victoria, 3192 Australia
Email: info@halleonard.com.au

Come Alive

Arranged by
MARK BRYMER

Words and Music by BENJ PASEK
and JUSTIN PAUL

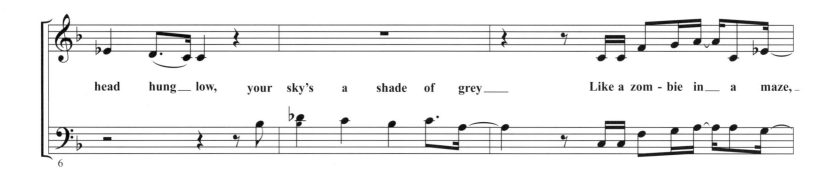

The Greatest Show

Arranged by
MARK BRYMER

Words and Music by **BENJ PASEK,
JUSTIN PAUL and RYAN LEWIS**

Driving, with swagger ($\bullet$ = ca. 78)

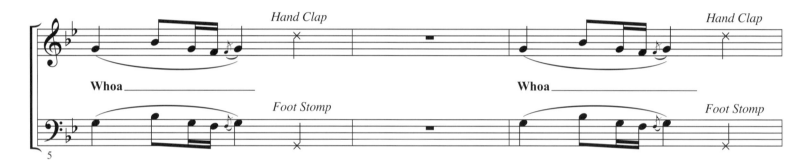

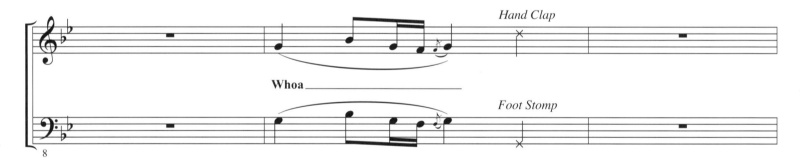

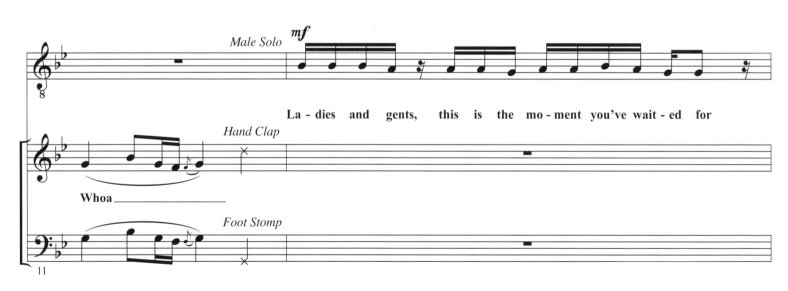

14

A Million Dreams

Arranged by
MAC HUFF

Words and Music by BENJ PASEK
and JUSTIN PAUL

day_____

day_____

They can say, they can say it all__ sounds cra-

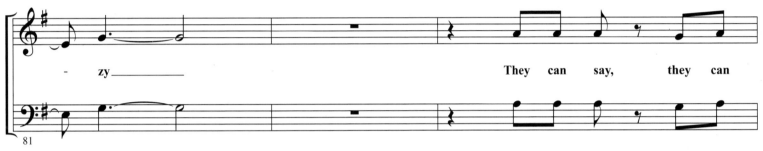

- zy_____

They can say, they can

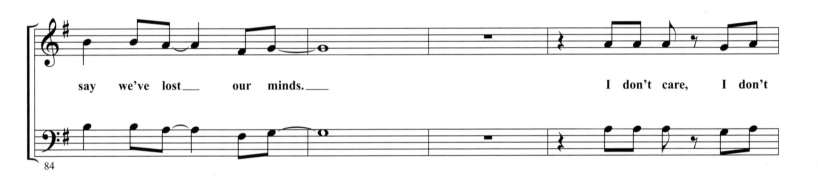

say we've lost__ our minds.__

I don't care, I don't

care if they call us cra - zy._____

Run a - way__ to a

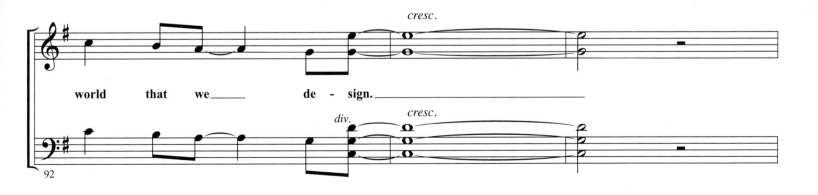

world that we_____ de - sign._____

24

Never Enough

Arranged by
MARK BRYMER

Words and Music by
BENJ PASEK and JUSTIN PAUL

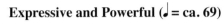

Nev - er   for me,___   for me___   Nev-er e - nough___

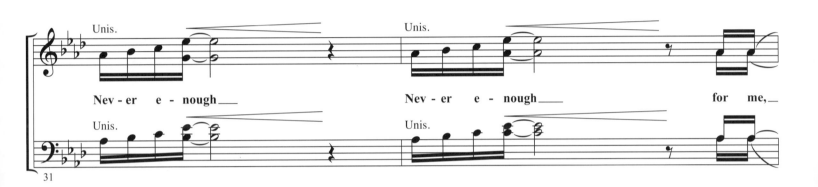

Nev - er e - nough___   Nev - er e - nough___   for me,___

Unis.   Unis.

Unis.   Unis.

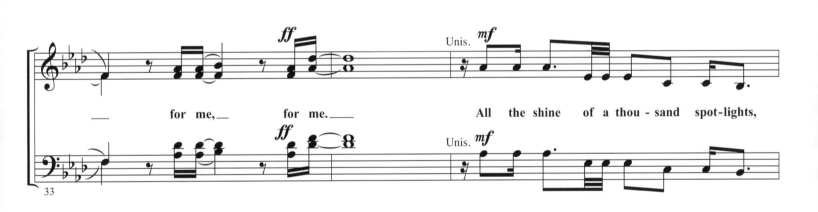

___   for me,___   for me.___   All the shine of a thou - sand spot-lights,

Unis.   Unis.

all the stars___ we steal___ from the night___ sky, will nev - er be e - nough,___

30

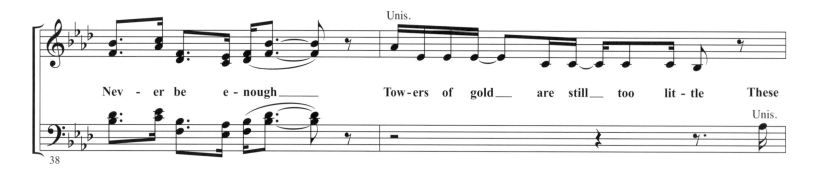

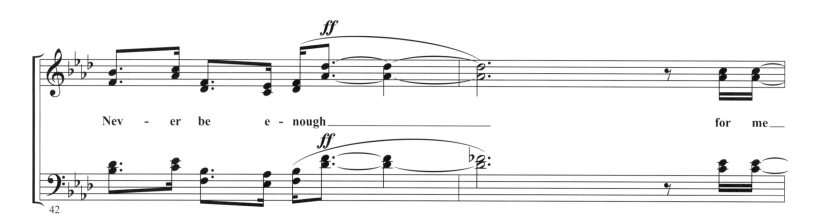

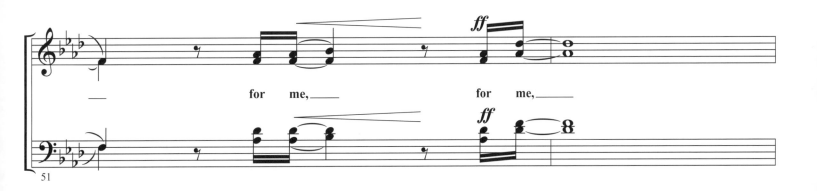

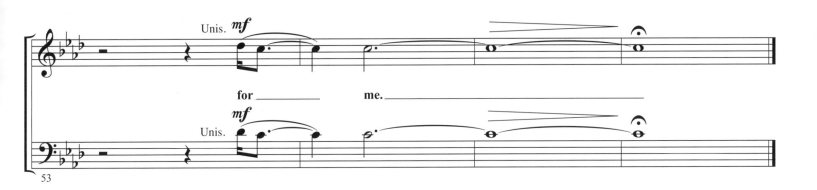

Rewrite the Stars

Arranged by
ROGER EMERSON

Words and Music by **BENJ PASEK**
and **JUSTIN PAUL**

Alto

You think I don't want to run_____ to you?_____

But there are moun - tains,_____ and there are doors that we can't_

cresc. poco a poco

___ walk through. _ I know you're won - der - in' why, be - cause we're a - ble to be_

___ just you and me with - in___ these_ walls.___ But when we go out - side_

you're gon - na wake up and see_____ that it___ was hope - less af - ter___ all.

end opt. Solo Soprano **f**

Alto

No one can re - write___ the stars_

Tenor
Unis. **f**

Bass

___ How can you say_____ you'll_ be mine?_____ Ev - 'ry - thing

Unis.

36

This Is Me

**Arranged by
MAC HUFF**

**Words and Music by BENJ PASEK
and JUSTIN PAUL**

When - ev - er the words_ wan-na cut me down I'll

____ a - pol - o - gies. This is me.

Eh   Eh

Oh_____

83

send a flood_ to drown 'em_ out_____   Oh,_____

Unis.

div.

Oh_____   Oh_____

Eh   Eh   Eh   Eh   Eh   Eh

Oh_____   Oh,_____

85

oh,_____   oh,_____   oh,   oh This is me.

Unis.

oh,_____   oh,_____   oh,   oh This is me.

88